Ben and Imo

Mark Ravenhill

methuen | drama
LONDON • NEW YORK • OXFORD • NEW DELHI • SYDNEY

METHUEN DRAMA
Bloomsbury Publishing Plc
50 Bedford Square, London, WC1B 3DP, UK
1385 Broadway, New York, NY 10018, USA
29 Earlsfort Terrace, Dublin 2, Ireland

BLOOMSBURY, METHUEN DRAMA and the Methuen
Drama logo are trademarks of Bloomsbury Publishing Plc

First published in Great Britain 2024

Cover design by RSC Visual Communications

Cover images: English composer and pianist Benjamin Britten
(1913–1976), circa 1949. (Photo by Alex Bender/Denis de Marney/Hulton
Archive/Getty Images); Imogen Holst © Brian Seed / Bridgeman Images

A catalogue record for this book is available from the British Library.

A catalog record for this work is available from the Library of Congress.

ISBN: PB: 978-1-3504-7160-3
ePDF: 978-1-3504-7162-7
eBook: 978-1-3504-7161-0

Series: Modern Plays

Typeset by Mark Heslington Ltd, Scarborough, North Yorkshire
Printed and bound in Great Britain

To find out more about our authors and books visit
www.bloomsbury.com and sign up for our newsletters.

OYAL
HAKESPEARE
OMPANY

ABOUT THE ROYAL SHAKESPEARE COMPANY

The Shakespeare Memorial Theatre was founded by Charles Flower, a local brewer, and opened in Stratford-upon-Avon in 1879. Since then, the plays of Shakespeare have been performed here, alongside the work of his contemporaries and of current contemporary playwrights. In 1960, the Royal Shakespeare Company as we now know it was formed by Peter Hall and Fordham Flower. The founding principles were threefold: the Company would embrace the freedom and power of Shakespeare's work, train and develop young actors and directors and, crucially, experiment in new ways of making theatre. The RSC quickly became known for exhilarating performances of Shakespeare alongside new masterpieces such as *The Homecoming* and *Old Times* by Harold Pinter. It was a combination that thrilled audiences, and this close and exacting relationship between writers from different eras has become the fuel that powers the creativity of the RSC.

In 1974, The Other Place opened in a tin hut on Waterside under the visionary leadership and artistic directorship of Buzz Goodbody. Determined to explore Shakespeare's plays in intimate proximity to her audience and to make small-scale, radical new work, Buzz revitalised the Company's interrogation of the relationship between the contemporary and classical repertoire. This was followed by the founding of the Swan Theatre in 1986 – a space dedicated to Shakespeare's contemporaries, as well as later plays from the Restoration period, alongside living writers.

In nearly 60 years of producing new plays, we have collaborated with some of the most exciting writers of their generation. These have included: Edward Albee, Howard Barker, Alice Birch, Richard Bean, Edward Bond, Howard Brenton, Marina Carr, Lolita Chakrabarti, Caryl Churchill, Martin Crimp, Can Dündar, David Edgar, Helen Edmundson, James Fenton, Georgia Fitch, Robin French, Juliet Gilkes Romero, Fraser Grace, David Greig, Tanika Gupta, Matt Hartley, Ella Hickson, Kirsty Housley, Dennis Kelly, Hannah Khalil, Anders Lustgarten, Tarell Alvin McCraney, Martin McDonagh, Tom Morton-Smith, Rona Munro, Richard Nelson, Anthony Neilson, Harold Pinter, Phil Porter, Mike Poulton, Mark Ravenhill, Somalia Seaton, Adriano Shaplin, Tom Stoppard, debbie tucker green, Frances Ya-Chu Cowhig, Timberlake Wertenbaker, Peter Whelan and Roy Williams.

The RSC is committed to illuminating the relevance of Shakespeare's plays and the works of his contemporaries for the next generation of audiences and believes that our continued investment in new plays and living writers is a central part of that mission.

The work of the RSC is supported by the Culture Recovery Fund

New Work at the RSC is generously supported by Hawthornden Foundation and The Drue and H.J. Heinz II Charitable Trust

The RSC Acting Companies are generously supported by The Gatsby Charitable Foundation

NEW WORK AT THE RSC

We are a contemporary theatre company built on classical rigour. Through an extensive programme of research and development, we resource writers, directors and actors to explore and develop new ideas for our stages, and as part of this we commission playwrights to engage with the muscularity and ambition of the classics and to set Shakespeare's world in the context of our own.

We invite writers to spend time with us in our rehearsal rooms, with our actors and creative teams. Alongside developing new plays for all our stages, we invite playwrights to contribute dramaturgically to both our productions of Shakespeare and his contemporaries, as well as our work for, and with, young people. We believe that engaging with living writers and contemporary theatre-makers helps to establish a creative culture within the Company which both inspires new work and creates an ever more urgent sense of enquiry into the classics.

Shakespeare was a great innovator and breaker of rules, as well as a bold commentator on the times in which he lived. It is his spirit which informs new work at the RSC.

Support us and make a difference; for more information visit
www.rsc.org.uk/support

This production of *Ben and Imo* was first performed by the Royal Shakespeare Company in the Swan Theatre, Stratford-upon-Avon, on 21 February 2024. The cast was as follows:

SAMUEL BARNETT	**BEN**
VICTORIA YEATES	**IMO**
RICHARD KEIGHTLEY	**UNDERSTUDY BEN**
ISABELLA MARSHALL	**UNDERSTUDY IMO**

CREATIVES

WRITER	**MARK RAVENHILL**
DIRECTOR	**ERICA WHYMAN**
DESIGNER	**SOUTRA GILMOUR**
LIGHTING DESIGNER	**JACKIE SHEMESH**
MUSIC	**CONOR MITCHELL**
SOUND DESIGNER	**CAROLYN DOWNING**
MOVEMENT DIRECTOR	**LUCY CULLINGFORD**
DRAMATURG	**PIPPA HILL**
CASTING DIRECTOR	**MATTHEW DEWSBURY CDG**
MUSIC DIRECTOR	**CONNOR FOGEL**
VOICE AND TEXT	**LIZ FLINT**
ASSISTANT DIRECTOR	**GABRIELLA BIRD**
PRODUCTION MANAGER	**LUCY GUYVER**
COSTUME SUPERVISOR	**CHRIS CAHILL**
COMPANY MANAGERS	**PIP HOROBIN** **SUZANNE BOURKE**
STAGE MANAGER	**LINDSEY KNIGHT**
DEPUTY STAGE MANAGER	**ALEX BURKE**
ASSISTANT STAGE MANAGER	**CHLOE-DANIELLE ROBSON**
PRODUCER	**SARAH-KATY DAVIES**

MUSICIAN

PIANO	**CONNOR FOGEL**

This text may differ slightly from the play as performed.

Ben and Imo

Characters

Benjamin Britten
Imogen Holst

*The play is set in Benjamin Britten's work room in Crag House,
Aldeburgh.*

1952

One

Imo Help? No. You mustn't help me. I'm here to help you.

Ben Help you find somewhere to stay.

Imo I've found somewhere to stay.

Ben Just like that?

Imo Just like that.

Ben Somewhere to stay tonight?

Imo Somewhere to stay for nine months.

Ben Imo!

Imo That's how long you've got, isn't it? To write the opera.

Ben Your job at Dartington.

Imo Packed it in. When you telephoned. I said goodbye Dartington and came to Aldeburgh as soon as I could. I didn't altogether fit in at Dartington. I was a puzzle. My students – excellent results and yet I never stuck to the curriculum. That pissed off the pen people. What am I to be called?

Ben I hadn't thought.

Imo What is my role? I don't mean billing. You can leave my name off anything you want. But what is the part that I'm to play in the making of the opera? So I don't over step the mark.

Ben I don't see how you can.

Imo Oh I can. I can over step the mark awfully. That's why a title's important. Keep me in line.

Ben   Where are you staying?

Imo   Not so far away.

Ben   When your stuff arrives.

Imo   It's arrived.

Ben   When did it arrive?

Imo   Here. With me. Now.

Ben   Three bags. Your stuff is three bags?

Imo   Once upon a time I could get everything into one bag. May I put my coat on here?

Ben   Of course.

Imo   I read *Elizabeth and Essex* on the train.

Ben   I've barely looked at my copy.

Imo   I've marked up what I think are the key scenes. We can work from my copy. Of course my markings – only my first, random impressions. To get a grip of the story.

Ben   I don't want you working on the libretto.

Imo   I see.

Ben   Just the musical side of things.

Imo   But if one isn't engaged with the words how can one ever –?

Ben   Yes?

Imo   No. Line over stepped. Mouth shut. But. What is my role to be?

Ben   Do you like the story?

Imo   I should say: It doesn't matter if I like the story.

Ben   I want to know. Is Elizabeth and Essex the right subject?

Imo   It's your subject. How about musical assistant? Would that sum up the role I'm to play? Surely that will do it? Musical assistant.

Ben   Sounds menial.

Imo   Then what?

Ben   Drink?

Imo   Just a small one for me. I can't take it like I used to. Young woman: I'd drink a bottle of wine and then be at the piano at eight the next morning but now I –

Ben   I'm the same.

Imo   You? Still a young man.

Ben   Only a few years younger than you. Thirty nine. Cheers.

Imo   Cheers. I'm an old spinster. If I'm going to get everything done, if you're going to write *Gloriana* in time for the coronation gala, then I shall have to be jolly careful with the drink.

Ben   Will you make sure that I'm jolly careful with the drink?

Imo   I shan't be a gaoler. I shall confine myself – as you have suggested – solely to matters musical. Assisting with the music. I wonder . . .

Ben   What?

Imo   Why you chose me. To be your . . . whatever I am.

Ben   Ah well. I didn't want anyone at all.

Imo   I was forced upon you?

Ben   Harewood gave me a stiff talking to. I couldn't take on such a huge undertaking by myself. I got cross with him. I get cross an awful lot – you'll have to watch out for that – told him to fuck off. There was no one I could trust to be so close to me when I was composing.

Imo   I understand. I can leave now if you'd rather.

Ben   No no.

Imo   If someone will drive me to Sax.

Ben   Last train's gone.

Imo   I can sleep on a bench and catch the early.

Ben   To where?

Imo   Ah. There you have me. Homeless. Well there's mother, only . . . mothers are the hardest work of all.

Ben   Harder than composers? I lay awake in the bed for hours and I turned to Peter – woke him up – and I said: What am I to do? Is there anyone I can allow to work alongside me on *Gloriana*? And Peter said: You've got to have Imogen Holst. She's quite brilliant and I said: By God you're right, she is, it has to be Imo.

Imo   Oh Ben. How thrilling! Did Harewood say what I was to be called?

Ben   Maybe. I don't recall. When the rage descends I don't catch much.

Imo   Is Ronnie Duncan on libretto?

Ben   God no. I couldn't put myself through Ronnie Duncan again. Plomer.

Imo   Plomer? Well. That's good.

Ben   Is it?

Imo   Definitely. Plomer will do well. With guidance.

Ben   Is there anything good I wonder about writing an opera for the coronation? I've banged on about a national opera. British national opera. And now they've come to wave it in my face. Look now we've got an Arts Council. Covent Garden. Royal coronation gala. Everything here for

Benjamin Britten's national opera. Now Benjamin Britten better bloody well write one.

Imo   Don't you want to write *Gloriana*? If you don't now's the last chance. Ditch it.

Ben   I couldn't.

Imo   Write whatever you most want to write.

Ben   I can't.

Imo   Why?

Ben   The public schools of England. They drill it in to one: duty duty duty. Damn them! I can't tell anymore. Am I writing *Gloriana* for art of for duty? I'll only know when I've done the bloody thing and if it's duty it will be the dullest opera you can imagine. I get so ill. When I have to write. Aches all over, pains tearing through.

Imo   My father was the same. I've been through it all before. You don't scare me.

Ben   You seem very sure of that.

Imo   I am. My father was always impressed. I'm a very good composer's assistant. I brought you a present.

Ben   Imo. You shouldn't have.

Imo   To thank you for bringing me to Aldeburgh. No wrapping. That would be silly. Here.

Imo *gives* **Ben** *a book.*

Imo   You haven't read it already have you?

Ben   Ah. I meant to –

Imo   But then you probably know everything about my father that you need to know.

Ben   I'll read it now.

Imo   Save it until *Gloriana*'s done.

Ben   Book writing, Imo. That's hard work.

Imo   I started writing it as soon as Holst died. I felt I must get it down while his memory was fresh. It carried me through five years. Sometimes writing it I felt I was more him than I was me. When I finished it – horrible. But there we are. The living go on.

Ben   You must sign it.

Imo   Oh yes! Sign it! Yes! I haven't a pen!

Ben   Here.

Imo   What shall I write?

Ben   Write: For Ben with love from Imogen September 1952.

Imo   Love from feels rather forward.

Ben   Write it all the same.

Imo   You think? (*Writes.*) Love from Imogen.

Ben   Imo. When do you think you'll die?

Imo   Gosh. What a question!

Ben   Don't you think about it? Ever?

Imo   My own death? No. I thought a lot about Gussie dying.

Ben   Gussie?

Imo   It's better than Gustav. I thought about Gussie dying then Gussie did die. And it was awful. But with composers it's different. There's still Gussie's music.

Ben   You're a composer, Imo.

Imo   I can make arrangements.

Ben   An evening at the Wigmore Hall entirely of your own compositions. You're a composer. Say it: I'm a composer.

Imo   Stop that!

Ben I'm a composer.

Imo Stop right now!

Ben Why?

Imo I'm not good enough.

Ben Says who?

Imo Says me. A composer is a very special thing like Gussie or you. I'm just not one of those special people. I don't know quite know what I am. Which is I suppose why – sorry – I keep banging on about what is my role in the making of *Gloriana*?

Ben What do you want it to be, Imo?

Imo I suppose . . . I'm a helper. I helped Gussie to compose and now I'm here to help you compose.

Ben We can't call you 'helper' in the gala programme book, June the eighth.

Imo I'm happy with musical assistant.

Ben I went to see my lawyer today and he said to me: The most likely thing is that you and Peter will die together in a plane crash.

Imo Well, there's cheerful!

Ben His way of saying I suppose that Peter and I will always be together. Even in death.

Imo Do you believe that?

Ben No. One day Peter will find the right girl. Off he'll go. Get married. I shall just have to lump it, won't I?

Imo Maybe you'll be the one to find the right girl.

Ben And maybe you'll find the right boy, Imo.

Imo Oh I tried. Matters of the heart, the body. At the time it was all rather wonderful. My twenty-fifth year, I decided to have a series of six photographs taken. In each of them I was in a different attitude from the dance. Like so and so and so and . . . I was entirely nude.

Ben   Well!

Imo   Each photo I gave to a different man. One of them wrote to me later. Called up to the war. He'd destroyed the photo as being 'unsuitable'. My body was so very beautiful. Then one day I just sort of knew that I was finished with all that, that I was to be a spinster from now on. Really, I've been very much happier ever since. My heart is still. Free to give my life to music. To composers. I was watching this evening.

Ben   Watching?

Imo   Watching you. Hid myself away at the back of the hall. Your choir practice for *Timon of Athens*.

Ben   It's still ragged.

Imo   I'd had – I'll confess it – some doubts on the train. Impulsive has got me in to trouble before. But when I saw you there, making music, the September light, I thought: Imogen Holst, you've done the right thing. Where else in the world could you possibly be than Aldeburgh? Gussie dreamed of a renaissance in English music. But still the composers wrote their careful little tone poems. Brahms with the wrong notes. But you. The renaissance. Shall we toast her?

Ben   Who?

Imo   Queen Bess.

Ben   How about amanuensis?

Imo   What?

Ben   Your role. We could call you: Amenuensis.

Imo   I don't like the sound of amanuensis at all.

Ben   Then what?

Imo   Tomorrow.

Ben   What am I to pay you?

Imo   Tomorrow. To *Gloriana*.

Ben *and* **Imo**   To *Gloriana*.

Two

Ben *is playing the entry music for Elizabeth from* Gloriana *on the piano.*

Ben (*calling out*)   And the trumpets!

He finishes.

Well, I think it's a start, isn't it? I mean there's a terrible danger with this sort of thing that one falls in to a pastiche. I want you to watch carefully for that and if you think I –

Imo   Oh no no no! (*She hugs him.*)

Ben   Oh.

Imo   Am I embarrassing you?

Pause.

Would you rather I let go?

Pause.

It's just sometimes the words won't – and only a –

Pause.

Only a jolly big hug will actually get the job done. I should let go.

Ben   Yes. You should. (*She does.*) What do you think of it? Honestly.

Imo   Honestly. I think it's marvellous.

Ben   Is it really alright?

Imo   Oh yes YES.

Ben   I thought if I could just get something down for the entrance of Elizabeth it would take the edge off the fear.

Imo   How's it doing – the fear?

Ben   Much better today, thank you. Oh Imo, I'm so grateful that you've listened.

Imo   Oh come off it.

Ben   No, honestly. That's what one needs. A few people who one really trusts.

Imo   Does Peter like it?

Ben   Peter hasn't heard it. You're the first.

Imo   The first of anyone to hear it?

Ben   The first of anyone to hear it.

Imo   That is the most thrilling thing that life can ever offer.

Ben   Oh Imo, I'm so happy!

Imo   Me too.

Ben   The first time in ages. Really happy. How long will it last?

Imo   Let's enjoy it while it's here. Happy!

Ben   Happy! When I'm writing Essex of course I hear Peter. Although Peter's a terribly reluctant Essex –

Imo   He'll be perfect.

Ben   Young lover, man of action – doesn't feel it's him.

Imo   Peter's very handsome.

Ben   There's handsomer.

Imo   Peter will be a wonderful Essex.

Ben   I have to write for Peter because that's what I know. When the libretto says Elizabeth, Queen of England and Essex, an earl in love with the Queen – I hear Joan Cross and Peter and that's the only way to do it.

Imo   Of course.

Ben   Covent Garden say –

Imo   Covent Garden – tch!

Ben   – oh you're writing for a clique.

Imo   Stuff Covent Garden.

Ben   And I say: How do you make art? Not with the pick of everything, shipped in from here and shipped in from there but with a few people you really –. With a – yes – clique.

Imo   Good for you.

Ben   Looking at it on the page I couldn't tell. Is it perhaps just an awful muddle of notes? Now playing it to you, it begins to make sense. Welcome to the clique.

Imo   Oh, I don't want. Maybe it's better . . .

Ben   Yes?

Imo   I'd rather. Don't count me in the clique. I'm a free sort of spirit. Very important. For me. Independence.

Ben   If that's what you want. I'll pull you in eventually.

Imo   You can try.

Ben   How do you like Aldeburgh? Are you settled?

Imo   That's not a word I'd use.

Ben   Everyone settles eventually.

Imo   I don't believe I'll ever settle. Not even eventually. During the war, I was sent to the West Country. Somerset. I'd move from village to village. Promoting the love of music. Never knew what would happen from one day to the next, whether I'd find a wonderful choir or a place which seemed completely disinterested in music of any kind. I'd unearth an old boy who remembered a folk song, which led someone else to remember another folk song and off we'd jolly well go. In a village school, a thousand feet above sea level, I heard the authentic tempo and phrasing of 'Up was I on my furrther's farm'. Often I didn't know where I was going to sleep. I was appointed because I allowed the committee to assume I had a car. I had a bicycle. I was terribly happy. The happiest I ever was. I'm a gypsy.

Ben   You won't gypsy away from Aldeburgh just yet will you, Imo?

Imo   Not just yet. There's *Gloriana*.

Ben   Not just *Gloriana*, there's . . .

Imo   Yes?

Ben   After *Gloriana* there's the festival. You must stay for the festival. Then the next. It goes on forever.

Imo   Forever?

Ben   And a day.

Imo   I'm not terribly good at forever and a day.

Ben   How about next year? You'll stay in Aldeburgh next year?

Imo   After *Gloriana*? No. Once *Gloriana*'s done I shall be back out in the world.

Ben   You should think about it. Join the committee. Help plan our festival for 1953.

Imo   I can't. Maybe – if there's the odd day or two when you don't need me.

Ben   Yes?

Imo   If I could work with amateurs. That's the real pulse of music.

Ben   And I'm – what? – a dead hand?

Imo   No. You're a genius. But that's pointless.

Ben   Ha!

Imo   There's no point is there in your being a genius without a community who love music, study music, make music.

Ben   Join the committee.

Imo   Stop it.

Ben   That's settled then.

Imo   I'd like to give it some thought.

Ben   Imogen Holst proposed for the planning committee for the Aldeburgh festival 1953. Objections? None. Show of hands? Unanimous. Carried. Welcome Imogen Holst to the planning committee Aldeburgh festival 1953.

Imo   Ben! You're a monster!

Ben   Yes, I am.

Imo   I shall decide if and when I'm on the committee. And if I'm on the committee I shall insist on some Holst in the programme.

Ben   That's it! Will you write something new for us?

Imo   I don't mean Imogen Holst.

Ben   No?

Imo   Of course not. I mean Gustav Holst. Have you read your book?

Ben   Which book?

Imo   My book about Gussie.

Ben   Oh that book. Yes, read it all the way through to the end.

Imo   What did you think? Honestly.

Ben   Much too short.

Imo   Too short?

Ben   Much too short. Must be hard when so many people are still alive. Much better if they're dead. Won't be too long and then we'll all die and you can tell the true story can't you?

Imo   I don't believe you read it very carefully. It's a very good book. Anyone who's really read it has said so. Could I hear Elizabeth's entrance just one more time?

Ben   Actually, no. I'm tired.

Imo   Alright.

Ben   Sorry.

Imo   Another time.

Ben   Good night.

Imo   Good night.

Pause.

Ben   Will I see you in the morning?

Imo   In the morning? No. As a matter of fact. No.

Ben   No?

Imo   No. I'm planning to go up to London in the morning.

Ben   But you're meant to be here in the morning. Running away to London?

Imo   It's Vaughan Williams' eightieth.

Ben   Really? So old and still so second rate.

Imo   Gussie and Vaughan were always so close and since Gussie isn't here I feel I ought to.

Ben   Will you come back?

Imo   Well of course I'll come back.

Ben   When will you come back?

Imo   I'll be back Friday.

Ben   Make sure you do. People have a tendency –

Imo   Yes?

Ben   They run away from me.

Imo   I shan't. At least not while there's *Gloriana* to be made.

Ben   You'll hear the lute songs and the recitative when you get back. If I'm not too horribly tired.

Imo   I'll give Vaughan Williams your best wishes.

Ben   I haven't sent them.

Imo   I know but I'll give them all the same.

Ben   Imogen Holst, I see what you're doing.

Imo   What am I doing?

Ben   You're keeping your distance.

Imo   Am I?

Ben   Keeping your distance. From me.

Imo   It's only a day in London.

Ben   Which is quite the right thing to do. You've worked me out.

Imo   I wouldn't say that.

Ben   You see how I am. What I do is . . . I find a person. I enchant the person. Throw a spell. Pull the person in closer, closer. Until they're in love with me. Don't fall in love with me. I think often I'm in love with them back. Then one day suddenly I despise them. Their weakness in being so easily enchanted. I try to push them away. Only they won't be pushed away. They're too deep in. Under the spell. So what

I have to do is I have to draw on my cruelty. Have to hurt
them so badly. I have to break them. It's the only way to
push them back from where they came. Do you see?

Imo   You paint a very dark picture of yourself.

Ben   It's a warning.

Imo   I know. And I understand. But all the same – you
won't get me.

Three

Ben *watches as* **Imo** *reads a letter.*

Ben   You see?

Imo   One minute more. When I've got to the end.

Ben   Hurry!

Imo   As fast as I . . .

Imo *reads to the end of the letter.*

Ah well.

Ben   Ah well? Is that all you've got to say? Ah well.

Imo   Maybe it's for the best.

Ben   The best?

Imo   *Gloriana* will still go ahead only –

Ben   But surely the whole point – the whole point / of
Gloriana –

Imo   Surely not / the whole point? Isn't the point?

Ben   The whole reason why I've dropped everything,
committed myself to this ridiculous schedule – grand opera
in nine months. The reason why you're here is because
Gloriana is for June the eighth. The coronation gala
performance at Covent Garden. This is why, why –

Imo   I know you're angry, dear.

Ben Too fucking right I'm angry!

Imo But Ben, if you'll only –

Ben Am I having a tantrum? Are you going to soothe me, Nanny Holst?

Imo I'm going to reason with you.

Ben Don't bother!

Imo I suppose what Kenneth Clark is saying –

Ben Kenneth Clark is a cunt.

Imo A cunt of course, but what he's saying –

Ben He's saying that they want to drop *Gloriana* for June the eighth.

Imo Yes dear.

Ben Replace it with a more popular piece. Some nineteenth century – Or, or, or – a ballet.

Imo Ballet! Lord! Where does he say ballet? Oh yes. Here. A ballet!

Ben Hopping around in their tulle doing their little spins when I've – oh! Fuck the ballet! Fuck Kenneth Clark! Fuck them all!

Imo Do you think possibly . . . Just possibly this might – don't look at me like that – Don't you . . . possibly . . . a gala night . . . a lot of royals . . . lady of the bedchamber . . . Sir Garter of the Household . . . All those show ponies . . . tails and gloves and tiaras . . . well, what I mean to say is aren't the royals a pretty frightful bunch? I mean what have gloves and tiaras to do with the wonderful local people who stood in this room just the other night singing Purcell? I suppose what I mean to say is: The royals are phoney and stupid and kitsch so let them have *Norma* or the Sugar Plum fucking Fairy. *Gloriana* can open a week or so later. A real audience. An opera audience not a / gala extravaganza.

Ben   No! No! New queen. National celebrations. New opera. My opera. *Gloriana*.

Imo   You're decided on that?

Ben   I'm very definitely decided on that.

Imo   What will you do? Write to Kenneth Clark? Motor up? If I can be of any help.

Ben   Help? How can you possibly help? What will you do? Telephone the Queen?

Imo   Don't be silly dear.

Ben   Imo, I do know. This will almost certainly fail.

Imo   I didn't say . . .

Ben   The royals and a new work. The worst audience. And I should say fine – do a little ballet. But I can't. Peter agrees with you but still I – Oh, why can't I walk away from it? But I won't.

Imo   Then I suppose it's my job to follow you wherever you go. Gosh! Listen to the sea. It rather reflects your mood.

Ben   My mood reflects the sea. Always does. I'll write to Clark. *Gloriana* must be presented on June the eighth.

Imo   Very well. You write to Clark now, I'll take the letter down to the post office before they shut shop. Shall I wait here while you write the letter or would you rather I –?

Ben   Do you want children?

Imo   Children? What has that got to –?

Ben   Do you?

Imo   I never think about it. The letter, dear.

Ben   Think about it now.

Imo   I'd rather not.

Ben   I think we might adopt a couple of children. Peter and I. There's camps in Germany. Misplaced persons. I'd like one boy and one girl. I don't suppose we should be allowed the girl. It's such a thoroughly male household, isn't it?

Imo   I suppose it is.

Ben   We'd be given two little boys.

Imo   Little boys would be alright. I mean I shouldn't want them but . . .

Ben   You should think about children. Of your own.

Imo   No thank you.

Ben   And marriage.

Imo   Marriage!

Ben   While you still can.

Imo   Gussie said towards the end: Imo, my best wish for you is that you should have a son or daughter who brings you the same joy that you have brought me. Which was a wonderful thing to say. But still . . . Benjamin Britten, will you please write that letter!

Ben   I don't suppose I shall ever get married. So there won't be any children that are properly my own. But I have a love for children. And it would be so awful to waste that. Without children, a person grows more and more selfish.

Imo   Am I grown more and more selfish?

Ben   I wasn't thinking of you.

Imo   Who then?

Ben   Me.

Imo   Then after *Gloriana* you must go to Germany and find your children.

Ben   When the liberation came, I drove through Germany. Misplaced peoples. Millions of them. After they opened up

Belsen, I went to play for the prisoners. With Yehudi Menuhin. When you see . . . What can you play? Everything we'd prepared – impossible.

Imo   It must have been horrible.

Ben   It was . . . there are no words. Now they're all saying Europe's healing. And things are blooming in Britain. Hey ho! New Elizabethan age. Nonsense. Any moment it could turn and all the darkness – back again.

Imo   We must make music. Especially in the darkness. The retreat from Dunkirk. I was conducting an amateur orchestra in Frome. The leading violinist's son was waiting for rescue. The other side of the Channel. Not for one instant did she let her concentration slip from the score. You must find the right school for your German boys. And you must teach them madrigals.

Ben   Or maybe I'll never adopt them. Who knows?

Imo (*at window*)   Look at the wagtails! Look at them! Come and look!

Ben *joins* **Imo** *at the window.*

Imo   Look at them fly – beautiful. Like a dance. Coming together. Changing direction. All in time. How do they do it, do you think? I suppose they send each other messages. How? Brain waves?

Ben   They don't need a conductor do they?

Imo   No! If only we were the same down here, stuck on the ground.

Ben   No more bloody conductors!

Imo   Ha! No more bloody conductors!

Imo *moves around the room, flapping her arms in imitation of a bird. Eventually* **Ben** *joins her. Their movements become more synchronised until it's like a dance.*

Together   No more bloody conductors. No more bloody conductors.

Imo *breaks off.*

Imo   The letter, dear.

Ben   You know, Imo: you're much more than a musical assistant.

Imo   Pen. Paper. Write. Then we can deal with the lute songs.

Four

Ben *and* **Imo**. **Ben** *with parcel.*

Ben   Surprise!

Imo   Oooooo!

Ben   By the last post.

Imo   What is it?

Ben   Published scores of Elizabethan music.

Imo   Thrilling!

Ben *opens the parcel.*

Ben   Inspiration for the Masque and the lute songs. (*Hands her a score.*) You start with this one and I'll start with this.

Imo   What are we looking for?

Ben   The Dowland *Lachrimae*.

They both study their scores for a while.

Imo   Gosh! The editing of this stuff! We have all this wonderful original Elizabethan music but in these dreadful editions. Somebody really has to do something about it.

Ben   You, Imo.

Imo   Well, if there's one thing I now how to do it's sorting out an awful mess like this. How can anyone work with these terrible –? Oh! Am I on my high horse? Why didn't you tell me to shut up? Honestly you must, soon as I start: Imo, shut up!

Ben   The lute songs for Essex. I thought study the Dowland Lachrimae. Get a feel for the thing. Should be a piano arrangement in here somewhere.

Imo   Look at the way this is – shut up, Imo!

Ben   Here it is!

Ben *begins to play the Dowland on the piano but after a while stops.*

Imo   What is it?

Ben   Nothing.

Tries again. Stops.

Ben   Damn arm. I get a pain. Shan't get the better of me.

Tries again, breaks off after a very short time.

Imo   I know the Dowland. You played it superbly but –

Ben   No, I'll –

Imo   Benjamin Britten, I forbid you to touch this piano! (*She closes the lid, hard.*) Now sit over there. And forget about playing just for a while and drink some wine.

She pours wine.

Ben   Knew this would happen. As soon as I start to compose – pain. I'm cursed.

Imo   I know all about this arm business. Gussie had it and was in terrible agonies and then I had it and the only thing to do is to stop. Drink your wine.

Ben   Doctor said it was all cured.

Imo   Well, you should go right back to him and tell him it's not.

Ben   I played tennis every day for the last three weeks, it didn't hurt.

Imo   You'll have to go easy on the tennis.

Ben   I like tennis.

Imo   There's an opera to be written!

Ben   Don't talk to me like that.

Imo   When you're being such a bloody fool, I'll talk to you exactly like that.

Ben   Did you talk to Holst like that?

Imo   Maybe I should have done. But I went off, my own way, didn't keep an eye on him night and day.

Ben   You are a gaoler! Well, maybe I won't stand for it. Maybe I'll send you packing. And then where will you go? Your post at Dartington's been filled. So you can't go back there.

Imo   More wine? (*Pouring.*) Might as well finish it off. I won't be sent packing. Any packing will be – I'll be own packer, thank you very much. I'll play the Dowland. Would you like that?

Ben   What? Even though the edition's terrible?

Imo   Indeed.

Imo *begins to play the Dowland. She's a very good pianist.*

Imo (*as she plays*)   The tuning on this old piano's awful. Shouldn't we have someone see to it?

Ben   I'm happy with it.

Imo   Then we'd better leave it be, hadn't we?

She continues playing.

Ben   Oh, Imo. Shut up and go back to your little house.
I'm ill.

Imo   I'll carry on, thank you very much.

Ben   For God's sake – stop!

He closes the piano lid with a bang.

Imo   Well, I think that's enough for today.

Ben   I think so too. You'd better stand further away from
me. I'm very down. If you're too close to me it will rub off on
you and you'll be down too. Sit right over there.

Pause.

You're not moving.

Imo   No.

Ben   I see.

Imo   It might happen the other way. Some of me might rub
off on you. I'll get really close to you – here – and let's see.

Pause.

Anything?

Ben   Of course not. Stupid game.

Imo   Gussie had the same. Blackness. I'm more of a getting
on with things sort of person. But then I'm not a genius. You
can't have genius without the blackness. Can you say what it
is that's depressing you?

Ben   Well, the opera of course. Stupid question.

Imo   Anything about the opera in particular?

Ben   So many things.

Imo   Has Clark replied? Have you been reinstated for the
royal gala?

Ben   Yes, Clark replied.

Imo   And?

Ben   *Gloriana*'s going ahead as the gala performance.

Imo   He's backed down?

Ben   He's backed down.

Imo   Really? Oh wonderful! / WONDERFUL!

Ben   Only – listen – LISTEN! – on one condition.

Imo   What condition?

Ben   He wants to give the ballet company a curtain raiser.

Imo   Well, I suppose the ballet company might –

Ben   No no no! *Gloriana* is an opera. It's not an item on a variety bill.

Imo   Did you tell that to Clark?

Ben   I told Clark to tell Dame Ninette to stuff her tulle up her backside.

Imo (*laughs*)   Oh Ben!

Ben   I told him he'll have to choose – for June the eighth – the ballet or *Gloriana*. He can't have both.

Imo   Which do you think he'll choose?

Ben   Probably the ballet.

Imo   Well at least you'll have all the other performances at Covent Garden.

Ben   Which is – you were right – much the best thing. Move away. I'm still very down.

Imo   Is it the Masque?

Ben   Ugh.

Imo   I knew it. It's the Masque.

Ben   Because really what am I going to do with all those dances? I can't see it. Elizabethans dancing.

Imo   Don't worry about the history. Old scores. Make them your dances. I know a fair bit about the – if you ever want me to dance. English folk dance, baroque – I've given demonstrations all over, Europe, America, even – Why don't I dance?

Ben   Here?

Imo   Here. You drink plenty of wine and I'll shake a leg with my English folk.

Ben   Imo, I'm stuck and depressed and will you stop being jolly about it because it's making it worse and it's actually – yes – making me ill! I didn't want you here in the first place. Only Harewood insisted. I knew it wouldn't work out.

Imo   Well, I'm here now so we just better jolly well make the most of it. I gave up a perfectly decent teaching post at Dartington. So I'm staying whatever you say. And you are going to write *Gloriana*. Understood? How's your arm?

Ben   Much better. Thank you.

Imo   Would you like to play me some of scene two?

Ben   No.

Imo   I want to hear it.

Ben   No. There's bits in scene two I'm still not sure about. If I play it now I'll only play it badly. That won't be any help to either of us.

Imo   Well. I don't suppose it shall.

A huge gust of wind shakes the building.

Gosh. Rain's coming in through this window frame. Look here. The carpet.

Ben   I've never noticed.

Imo   How can you not –?

Ben   That's what it's like here. Strangers find it hard to get used to.

Imo   It can't be good for you. Please let me help me with the dances.

Ben   We'll see.

Five

Ben *is showing* **Imo** *his manuscript score.*

Ben   And then there's the trumpets. On stage.

Imo   How many trumpets on stage?

Ben   I should say . . . three trumpets on stage.

Imo   Three? That's not an awful lot. Are you sure three?

Ben   Yes, I'm sure three.

Imo   You don't seem to be awfully sure about three trumpets.

Ben   Well, one doesn't want to ask Covent Garden for too much.

Imo   You should ask Covent Garden for as much as you jolly well want. It's your opera.

Ben   Yes, but still, you know . . . budgets and everything, one doesn't like to –

Imo   They'll be spending a fortune on the whole silly coronation business so at least they can give you –

Ben   Put it down as three trumpets.

Imo   No. Shan't. In your head you can hear it. So honestly, honestly, honestly . . . how many trumpets do you hear on stage? Honestly.

Ben   Twelve. Don't write that down.

Imo   It's already noted.

Ben   Twelve trumpets! I can't ask for twelve trumpets.

Imo   Yes you jolly well can ask for twelve trumpets and the tax payer can jolly well pay for it. That's what public art means.

Ben   Well, I suppose we could have twelve trumpets at the gala performance –

Imo   That's the spirit!

Ben   And then for the subsequent performances after the gala we could slim things down a bit.

Imo   Let's see about that. Now I'd like you to take a look at this. (*Gives him book.*) It's French. A dance treatise. But it's the right period. Should give you something to start with for the Masque.

Ben   Oh dances! (*He throws the book away from him.*)

Imo   Don't damage the book. It's on loan. And it's very old.

Ben   Let's play Happy Families.

Imo   I think we should push on. I'd like you to look at this. I've been working on –

But **Ben** *is already getting the pack of cards out of a drawer.*

Ben   This is a very old pack that I was first given when I was sent off to school. I'd sit and play Happy Families with myself after lights out. Will you divide the pack or shall I?

Imo   What if I don't want to play Happy Families?

Ben *divides the pack.*

Imo   I went to Oxford yesterday.

Ben   Oxford?

Imo   I've an old friend in Oxford who yesterday gave me some dance lessons so that I could come back here and dance for you. The Pavane, Galliard, La Volta. Elizabethan court dances. I thought it might get you moving along with the Masque.

Ben   Mr Mug the Milkman?

Imo   Would you prefer to look at the dances tomorrow?

Ben *starts to play Happy Families by himself.*

Imo   I've written up the act one scene one vocal score. Look at the state of your desk. Tomorrow I can tidy the whole thing up for you.

Ben   No thanks. Everything's just where I want it to be.

Imo   I have a comment on the score. Is it alright if I make comments? Only we've never established . . . am I simply to copy into neat or am I also to comment . . . because I'm sure some composers . . .

Ben   What is it? Out with it.

Imo   This phrase here. I was copying it and –

Ben   Which phrase?

Imo   Just here. You see, I've copied the phrase just as you wrote it but actually to me . . . my ear . . .

Ben   Yes?

Imo   It just sounds all wrong. 'Hath made us brothers' with the rise in the voice, you see? (*With a rising inflexion.*) 'Hath made us brothers.' Rather odd. Which is maybe what you wanted. Wanted it odd. But the actual, the more natural would actually be . . . (*With a lower inflexion on 'brothers'.*) 'Hath made us brothers.' You see, if I were to say it or indeed I think if most or all people were to say it 'Hath made us brothers'. . . do you see?

Ben   . . . Well.

Imo   And what do you think? Do you agree with me?

Ben   I don't know. I'd like to think about it if I may. 'Odd' or 'natural' . . . I don't know which I . . .

Imo   Yes, yes.

Pause.

Imo   I do hope I haven't over . . .

Pause.

Imo   This east wind. Finds its way in through all the cracks, doesn't it?

Ben   It gets worse. Winter's only just beginning. Imo.

Imo   Yes?

Ben   The blackness. It isn't shifting.

Imo   I know.

Ben   How long did it go on with Holst?

Imo   Sometimes I could cheer him up but other times . . .

Ben   Would you mind holding me for a while?

Imo   Holding you?

Ben   As a way . . . I think it might . . . draw off the depression. If you sit and then I curl up and put my head on your lap.

Imo   That's . . .

Ben   Not the job of a musical assistant?

Imo   No, I don't suppose it is.

Ben   But how am I to write if nothing draws off the depression? Did you hold Holst?

Imo   With Gussie no. Still a Victorian. I mustn't be drawn in. You mustn't pull me in too close.

Ben   Just to ease a little the darkness.

Imo *sits and* **Ben** *curls up and puts his head in her lap.*

Ben   That's it. And now sort of put your arms there and there. That's it. Comfortable?

Imo   Yes, thank you. You?

Ben   Oh yes, very good, thank you.

Pause.

If you could stroke my hair.

Imo   Don't be silly.

Pause.

Imo   The last two years of Gussie's life . . . I was still making my way in the world . . . rushing . . . I couldn't see . . . Mother wasn't the person. I should have been there. Beside him, making up his bar lines. Didn't mean to be but I was very cruel. I abandoned him.

Ben   I thought I'd caused my mother's death. Punished myself. But one day I realised – it wasn't me. We don't kill our parents. Not as much as we think we do.

Imo *begins to stroke* **Ben**'s *hair.*

Ben   When I was a child composing was easy. None of these hang ups. I've got whole stacks of scores I wrote when I was fifteen.

Imo   You've kept them?

Ben   In the cabinet there.

Imo *rises.*

Ben   What are you doing?

Imo   I must see them.

Ben   You're supposed to be holding me.

Imo   I want to look at your music.

Imo *takes a bundle of papers out of a cabinet.*

A treasure trove!

Imo *eagerly studies the manuscripts.*

Tell me about them, dear. Come over here. Look at all this.

Ben *joins her and they look at the manuscripts.*

Ben   It just came pouring out of me without all the . . . consciousness. It really is such a very blessed thing to be a child. But at some point you have to grow up. That's when all the troubles begin. Why is everyone in such a hurry to grow up nowadays? I'm sure we never grew up as fast as all that.

Imo   I grew up pretty fast.

Ben   You poor thing!

Imo   At least I thought I had. I met the man I wanted to marry when I was fifteen.

Ben   Really? And whatever happened to him?

Imo   This work needs to be catalogued.

Ben   You think so?

Imo   The earliest works of Benjamin Britten. Yes. Definitely. Catalogued.

Ben   You should catalogue them, Imo.

Imo   When would I have the time to catalogue them?

Ben   You'll have time after *Gloriana*.

Imo   There's the 1953 Aldeburgh festival after *Gloriana*.

Ben   You're staying for 1953?

Imo   I thought I might.

Ben   Aha!

Imo   But I shall need to move on after the 1953 festival.

Ben   Yes, of course.

Ben *inspects his juvenilia.*

Ben   When I was fifteen I went to London and I heard the *Planets*.

Imo   Did you like it?

Ben   I was thrilled. So inspired and I rushed home and I put a discord in to the symphony I was writing – just – here! – you see?

Imo   Oh yes! Gussie would be so proud.

Ben   Imo.

Imo   Yes?

Ben   I really am very grateful for everything.

Imo   There's no need.

Ben (*with a lower inflexion on 'brothers'*)   Hath made us brothers. Hath made us brothers. You're right of course. Hath made us brothers.

Imo   I'll make a note to remind you. Hath made us brothers.

Ben   Imo.

Imo   Yes?

Ben   Would you show me a dance?

Imo   Now?

Ben   Now. An Elizabethan dance you learned in Oxford.

Imo   Really?

Ben   Really.

Imo   Yes! Which shall I show first? Got it! A galliard! The Dowland 'Earl of Essex'.

Imo *pulls a score from her bag, passes it to* **Ben**, *who takes it to the piano.*

Ben   Incredible! Dowland wrote an Earl of Essex galliard?

Imo   I thought you'd like that. It's a partnered dance and of course I haven't a partner. So in some places I shall dance the woman, in some the man. Which I hope doesn't make a nonsense of the whole thing. The piano's not an instrument suited to dance but we must – oh come on, Imo, get on with it.

Imo *takes up her starting position.*

Ben   Ready?

Imo   Ready.

Ben *plays the galliard. A piece of about two minutes.* **Imo** *dances very well. Finishes with a man's bow.*

Ben   Bravo bravo! You really are a terribly good dancer, Imo.

Imo   Yes well, I told you I was.

Ben   But until one actually sees it –

Imo   Elizabeth the First kept up the dance well in to her later years – so I suppose I shall be able to continue for some time yet – Do you think it was of any use to you? What did you like?

Ben   I think . . . the cross rhythm in the galliard.

Imo   Oh yes, the cross rhythm – that's very Benjamin Britten.

Ben   Is it? What's that? What's 'very Benjamin Britten'?

Imo   It would be bliss if you used a galliard in *Gloriana*. And I thought you might – only if you want to – I had a vision.

Ben   A vision?

Imo   A child, their face painted, runs on to the stage and dances a Morris.

Ben   A small boy?

Imo   A small boy. What do you think?

Ben   A small boy in the middle of the pageantry. I like it very much.

Imo   Well, that's good.

Ben   But you mustn't fight me for him. He's all mine now. Let him go, Show me a Morris, Imo.

Imo   Now?

Ben   Now.

Imo   I'm not sure I'm altogether ready.

Ben   Now.

Imo *dances a Morris.*

Six

Ben *is wrapped in a blanket.*

Imo   Oh my dear. You look just awful. Has the doctor been?

Ben   This is just the start. I'll be ill for months now.

Imo   Shall I go away? When I'm ill, I don't want any company. I just hide myself away. Wait till it's all over. But I suppose you don't mind company.

Ben   It all depends on the company, doesn't it?

Imo (*producing flask*)   Brandy, honey and lemon. Piping hot. To get you better.

Ben   Peter says he's sure that Essex isn't his part.

Imo   I see.

Ben   Says it makes him sick with fear just to think about it.

Imo   I suppose if he really is so uncomfortable with the role –

Ben   He'll have to make himself comfortable.

Imo   How should he do that?

Ben   He should let me be the judge. I know Peter better than he knows himself.

Imo   But if he really doesn't want to play Essex. We should look at other possibilities.

Ben   Such as?

Imo   Such as Nicola Rossi-Lemeni.

Ben   Bleugh.

Imo   Is that such a bad idea?

Ben   It's a terrible idea.

Imo   His Boris last week was an absolute sensation.

Ben   I don't want sensations. I don't suppose your sensational Boris even has English.

Imo   I'm sure with coaching he can –

Ben   Huh!

Imo   Ben, dear. Peter doesn't like the whole idea of a coronation opera. Never has. He doesn't want to play Essex. What's the point in forcing him?

Ben   Peter will do as I say.

Imo   Are you sure that's best?

Ben   Very few people know what's best for them. Most people need their decisions made by someone else. And when it comes to Peter my decisions are better than his decisions.

Imo   He'd rather play Cecil.

Ben   Cecil isn't for him.

Imo   Essex is such a young character, man of action. Peter –

Ben   Will play Essex and he will come to learn that Essex is absolutely the right role for him.

Imo   Are you really sure you're the best judge? You're in love with Peter.

Ben   What's being in love with Peter got to do with it?

Imo   So maybe you look at him. See Essex the handsome lover wooing his Queen. Whereas others can see in Peter – Cecil, the counsellor, confidante –

Ben   If Peter won't take Essex then I won't finish the score.

Imo   Don't say that.

Ben   Peter didn't want to be a singer in the first place. Until I used the power of my persuasion. He may have been happier not being a singer. Who knows? But if he hadn't been a singer he'd have denied so many other people's happiness and that's what matters isn't it?

A coughing fit. **Imo** *pours brandy from the flask and gives it to* **Ben**.

Ben   There's more trouble with Ninette de Valois.

Imo   Oh no. What now? Has Clark chosen the ballet over your opera?

Ben   No decision yet from Clark about June the eighth.

Imo   Then what?

Ben   Little Dame Ninette wants Frederick Ashton to stage the dances in the *Gloriana* Masque.

Imo   Frederick Ashton? Would that be so terrible?

Ben   I want John Cranko for the dances in the Masque.

Imo   But maybe you could give Fredrick Ashton a go. He's terribly good.

Ben   No no no! I won't work with strangers. I want Cranko. I've got to have Cranko.

He has another huge coughing fit.

Imo   Now look what you've done.

Ben   We're going to London. You and I. Have it out with Dame Ninette.

Imo   When?

Ben   Tomorrow.

Imo   Are we? Let's see how you are in the morning.

Ben   Ashton has got to be sorted.

Imo   But not if you're like this.

Ben   We're going to be driven up in the Rolls.

Imo   You'll make yourself terribly ill.

Ben   For God's sake, stop trying to be my mother. You're not my mother and I won't be –

Another huge coughing fit.

Imo   I don't want to be anyone's mother but if you won't listen to kindly advice, what am I to do?

Ben   What can you do? What you can do is get in the bloody car and come to bloody London.

Imo   I only wish your own mother had been all together stricter with you. Then maybe you wouldn't behave so much like a spoilt child every time you don't get your own way.

Ben   Huh.

Pause.

Imo   The sea's particularly savage this morning. Like she really does want to gobble all of us up.

Ben   It's the work that makes me ill. Every bar, every . . . F natural is some sort of ache somewhere. Why have I got this flu?

Imo   Because it's December, freezing cold and you don't take care of yourself.

Ben   Because I'm worried about the Masque scene. All your showing me your galliard will go to waste. I won't be able to write at all if I think it's going to end up in the hands of Freddie Ashton. So if I'm going to get better –

Imo   Well, well.

Ben   Then I need to go up to London and sort the whole thing out. But I'm terribly weak. So I need you to help me. Isn't that what you're here for? To help.

Imo   Seems as though I don't have any choice.

More coughing.

I'm sorry. I seem to be very low on sympathy today.

Ben   I suppose people think that composing must be like being possessed by a great joy. Or they think it's a huge act of suffering. If only they knew what it was like. This continual dull ache. You will come to London with me, won't you?

A great roar from the sea.

Imo   Listen to that sea. So savage.

Ben   I can go on my own, you know.

Imo   Then do it. Go on your own.

Ben   I can't.

Imo   Then don't say you can.

Ben   I need you, Imo.

Imo   I know you do.

Ben   What would I do without you?

Seven

Ben *and* **Imo** *both work silently for a while on the score.*

Imo   I thought tomorrow in the morning.

Ben   I'm away with Peter tomorrow.

Imo   I see. Alright then the day after tomorrow.

Ben   The day after tomorrow is Christmas Day.

Imo   Is it? Christmas Day? The day after tomorrow? I suppose it is.

Ben   That's why I'm away with Peter. Until New Year. Ten days. For the holidays. See you in 1953.

Imo   Ten days with no work on *Gloriana*?

Ben   That's right.

Imo   Where are you going?

Ben   We're staying with George and Marion at Harewood.

Imo   Of course. I should have thought. I mean I suppose you were bound to go away for Christmas.

Ben   Where will you be?

Imo   Tomorrow?

Ben   The day after tomorrow. Christmas Day.

Imo   I hadn't actually thought because I supposed you might still be working over Christmas. If you told me you'd planned ten days away from *Gloriana*.

Ben   I can't remember to tell you everything I plan to do.

Imo   I don't expect you to. Only. Ten days. Well, we shall just have to double our efforts on *Gloriana* when you return. It really is very irresponsible to take off without telling me and abandon *Gloriana*.

Ben   Cross with me, Imo?

Imo   Furious.

She returns to her work.

Ben   You won't be on your own, Imo? For Christmas.

Imo   . . .

Ben   There's bound to be someone in Aldeburgh keep you company.

Imo   . . .

Ben   Imo?

Imo   I shan't stay in Aldeburgh.

Ben   Where then?

Imo   . . .

Ben   Where?

Imo   I shall go to stay with mother. Be good to remind her that I'm still alive.

Ben   You will come back to me though, Imo, won't you?

Imo   That's for me to know and you to find out.

Ben   David Webster came down yesterday. I thought checking on our progress on *Gloriana*. That's what I thought but – oh Imo, what am I to do?

Imo   Do about what, dear?

Ben   Webster said the most frightful things.

Imo   What sort of frightful things?

Ben   Frightful things about my duty to music in England.

Imo   I should say you're doing more than your duty to England.

Ben   Covent Garden's not right for opera – not for all opera – I mean Wagner is fat enough – but Mozart. It's no good for Mozart. And what point is an opera house that's not right for Mozart?

Imo   Where is this all heading, dear?

Ben   Webster's asked me to be musical director of Covent Garden.

Imo   I see.

Ben   What should I do?

Imo   What do you want to do?

Ben   I don't know.

Imo   Tell Webster that you'll think about it after *Gloriana*.

Ben   I tried that. He said I must decide tonight. Yes or no.

Imo   What a monstrous demand.

Ben   I'm not a conductor.

Imo   You are a conductor.

Ben   I'm not. Only for those I love. And then how would I find the time for my own composition? I can't be a public figure. I hate parties! Working in an office Monday to Friday.

Imo   It sounds to me that you've made your decision.

Ben   I haven't. I can't. Musical director of Covent Garden. There's a . . . lure. I want you to tell me what I want to do. Please.

Imo   After the first three years. Wandering Somerset, encouraging music wherever I went. I was exhausted. The council said to me: You are the greatest teacher of music we have. We'll put you in charge of six divisions. You will encourage music across the land. I was relieved at first. To sleep in my own bed. Then I realised that I wasn't amongst them. The evacuee mothers conducting with their hips while their babies beat the air with their fists, the grocer who led a madrigal choir in the sitting room behind the shop. I was at the end of a telephone and I was so so miserable.

Ben   Thank you, Imo.

Imo   For what?

Ben   For telling me what to do.

Imo   Ben, I don't believe that anyone has ever told you what to do.

Ben   I'll telephone Webster now.

Imo   What will you say?

Ben   I shall say: Bugger duty. I won't be musical director of Covent Garden.

Off recorders playing 'The Cherry Tree Carol'.

Ben   What's that?

Imo   The carollers are a-calling at your door. A surprise for you. My Christmas present. Not quite Christmas Day in the morning just yet but . . .

They listen for the a while.

Ben   Who's playing?

Imo   The children of Aldeburgh.

Ben   Who taught them?

Imo   Me. My amateurs.

Ben   The recorder arrangement.

Imo   From a baroque manuscript. I made some adjustments.

Ben   It's wonderful.

Imo   I'm very proud. Some of them have never played an instrument before. One of them made their own recorder.

A small children's choir joins the recorders.

Ben   The children's choir? You as well?

Imo   Yes, me.

Ben   You magicked them up?

Imo   I did it all the time during the war.

Ben   Aldeburgh's really pulled you in, hasn't she?

Imo   I won't be here a year from now. Christmas 1953 I shall be somewhere altogether different.

Ben   You won't.

Imo   I shall.

Ben   Where?

Imo   I don't know just yet.

Ben   Oh wonderful woman.

Ben *puts his arm around* **Imo** *and they listen with* **Imo**'s *right hand 'conducting' by her side.*

Carol (*off*)
    Then Mary said to Joseph
    So meek and so mild
    Pick me some cherries
    For I am with child.
    Then Joseph grew angry
    So angry grew he
    'Let the father of your baby
    Get the cherries for thee'.

Imo   Come and meet them. Put a penny in the hat.

Ben   Imo. First. I want to give you this. Happy Christmas.

Ben *hands* **Imo** *a wrapped present.*

The choir outside begin 'I Saw Three Ships'.

Imo   I didn't – you shouldn't have – can I unwrap it now? I know it's cheating only –

Ben   First I've prepared – I had to write it down or I shouldn't be able to say it (*Takes piece of paper from pocket, reads.*): Imo. It is quite impossible to thank you for what you've done and meant to me in these last months. Over and over again you've saved my sanity in so many different ways, by your energy, intelligence, infinite skill and affection. I give you this with my love. Ben. Open it now.

Imo *unwraps the present.*

Imo   Aha, *Billy Budd*! Thank you.

Ben   Look closer.

Imo   Your manuscript copy!

Ben   I don't have the printed edition.

Imo   Ben, no! I can't accept it.

Ben   I've given it you now.

Imo   I'm giving it back.

Ben   I won't take it back.

Imo   Please it's too – it's invaluable. I can't take it.

Ben   Imogen Holst, I order you to take possession of my manuscript of *Billy Budd*.

Imo   Oh Ben, I feel as though I've stolen it.

Ben   You haven't. You've earned it.

Imo   This will always be my most prized possession.

Pause.

Ben   Are you blubbing, Imo?

Imo   Just a little.

Ben   Do you want your carollers to see you've been blubbing?

Imo   No I jolly well don't.

Ben   Then we better.

Ben *takes his handkerchief, mops around* **Imo***'s eyes.*

Ben   By the way, Dame Ninette's backed down. I've got Cranko for the Masque.

Imo   Really?

Ben   And Kenneth Clark's given the ballet the boot. June the eighth. Our play is preferred. *Gloriana* will be the coronation gala performance.

Imo   Oh Ben!

Imo *kisses* **Ben** *impulsively on the lips.*

Ben   Yes, well. Now I've got to finish the fucking thing, haven't I?

(*Sings.*)
　　And all the souls on earth shall sing
　　On Christmas Day, on Christmas Day
　　And all the souls on earth shall sing
　　On Christmas Day in the morning.

Imo *joins him in descant.*

Ben/Imo
　　Then let us all rejoice again
　　On Christmas Day, on Christmas Day
　　Then let us all rejoice again
　　On Christmas Day in the morning.

1953

Eight

Ben Good God.

Imo Lucky I didn't go to mother after all isn't it?

Ben What happened?

Imo Christmas Eve. The winds just got fiercer and fiercer, rain like you've never seen and then just suddenly – here we were with the sea running in. Thank God I couldn't sleep so I rushed down here and started saving everything.

Ben How long did it take you?

Imo All night.

Ben You worked all through the night?

Imo Someone had to. Christmas morning I just collapsed, pulled my coat over me and slept on the piano.

Ben I need a drink.

Imo Careful. The carpet's still something of a swamp. Put these on. They're Mrs Hodson's so there might be a pinch.

Imo *hands* **Ben** *wellingtons which he puts on.*

Imo It's all rather spartan in here I'm afraid. Soon as the sun came out, I moved most of the furniture in to the garden. Just a few items so you can carry on with *Gloriana*. I knew you'd want the drinks tray ready for your return.

Ben Want one?

Imo Why not? Something stiff.

Ben Rum?

Imo   Drambuie for me. Thank goodness I ran down here
or everything would be washed away – oh not that much for
me.

Ben   Drink it. Well, happy new year. Here's to 1953.

Imo   To 1953.

They drink.

Ben   You don't think the flood is an omen, do you?

Imo   No I don't.

Ben   A curse upon *Gloriana*?

Imo   Oh shut up!

Ben   Everyone wants *Gloriana* to fail.

Imo   Everyone?

Ben   The newspapers.

Imo   Pff!

Ben   Half of them think the Arts Council is a foolish idea
and want *Gloriana* as a test case to prove what a silly waste it
is to spend public money on art.

Imo   Ignore them.

Ben   And the other thinks public money – good. But
Covent Garden? No. Why isn't public money going on work
made by the people for the people?

Imo   Drink your rum, dear.

Ben   Which is rather what you think isn't it, Imo?

Imo   Don't start on what I think or we'll be here all day. I've
done my best to mop and dry and heat but there – you can
still see – the mark on the wall – how high the water rose.

Ben   How's the piano?

Imo If anything I'd say it's a little less out of tune than it was before.

Ben *plays a phrase from* Peter Grimes *sea interlude on the piano.*

Ben Ha! You're right. My manuscript! Did the water come over my desk?

Imo I saved that first. Scooped up all the papers in a table cloth, got them up in the attic. Thank goodness they weren't in any order and could just be scooped. There's no electricity. Might be weeks they say.

Ben I shall compose by candlelight.

Imo Oh yes! Very Elizabethan. I like your coat.

Ben My Christmas present from Peter.

Imo May I touch it? Astrakhan? On anyone else it would look spivvy.

Ben Spivvy?

Imo But on you it's elegant.

Ben Where am I going to stay tonight?

Imo I've already spoken to the Potters. They were spared. So you're staying there.

Ben And you?

Imo I'm too high up to be affected.

Ben Tell you what, I'll come over to your place to eat tonight.

Imo I'm sure the Potters will be expecting you to –

Ben I suppose you can cook, can't you?

Imo Rather well, thank you.

Ben I'll be there at eight.

Imo It's not such a good idea. I've hardly got any room.

Ben   I don't need the Savoy. You've been here several months, seen every inch of my house. Don't you think it's time I saw yours?

Imo   No I don't!

Ben   Come on, Imo!

Imo   It's my room. Nobody comes in to my room.

Ben   Why ever not?

Imo   My privacy.

Ben   When did you become so private?

Imo   A long time ago. I'm a private person.

Ben   But you're so good with people.

Imo   I can act the part. I don't like people. Not really. I prefer crotchets and quavers.

Ben   Do you like me, Imo?

Imo   I like your music.

Ben   Peter's on tour. I should be with him. Harewood stopped me. For the good of *Gloriana*. Sent Noel Mewton-Wood to accompany Peter. Noel Mewton-Wood's efficient but . . . I'm lonely. I don't want to spend the evening with the Potters.

Imo   Well you must.

Ben   Why can't I come to you?

Imo   Because I've got nothing to cook on.

Ben   Nothing?

Imo   A single ring.

Ben   We'll have soup.

Imo   There's no table.

Ben   On our laps.

Imo   There's only one chair.

Ben   One chair?

Imo   One chair. The bed. And my Bach Gesselschaft.

Ben   And that's it?

Imo   And that's it. So now you know, you can see why . . . no supper. I've never been bothered by the routine of regular meals. Gussie's letters. 'Have you eaten today, Imo? I want you to be a little stouter next time we meet, Imo.' You're used to your life, Ben. You've earned every bit of it. But you mustn't assume that the rest of us live as you do.

Ben   I'll cook you something now.

Imo   There's no need.

Ben   I can scramble an egg.

Imo   I don't want you to scramble an egg. I should have been altogether firmer with you from the beginning. When it became clear that you weren't going to talk about money, I should have talked about money. But neither of us talked about money and so here I am muddling along still with no real idea of what my role is in the making of this bloody opera and no proper renumeration. Another Drambuie would be lovely.

Ben   Of course.

Ben *pours* **Imo** *another Drambuie and himself another rum.*

Ben   Imo. Are you really so awfully hard up?

Imo   At Dartington I was on a salary. So that was rather more comfortable. I liked the teaching but the administration, the continual ticking off about my teaching methods. Not the same as working with you is it?

Ben   But your room.

Imo   I'm not in my room that often. *Gloriana*, the amateurs, the festival office, lots of long walks. It's a place to sleep.

Ben   I thought with Holst's *Planets* being so popular. You should be comfortable. It must bring in lovely royalties.

Imo   All signed over to mother.

Ben   But you're the one who organised Holst's –

Imo   It's a perfectly sensible arrangement. I'm quite happy with it. I don't want to live on Gussie's royalties. What would that do to a person's mind? I want to make my own way in the world. Which I do. In my own fashion.

Ben   You mustn't martyr yourself, Imo.

Imo   Oh bugger off.

Ben   You're impossible!

Imo   Pot. Kettle. Black.

Ben   We really need to get you paid properly.

Imo   There was one thing I thought of.

Ben   Yes?

Imo   For money. A lecture tour of America. The Americans pay very well. I could tell them all about your work. Anywhere that you're played or about to be played, up I'd pop and tell the Americans all about you.

Ben   America?

Imo   If you'd help with introductions and letters of recommendation and things like that . . .

Ben   I'm not sure that Aldeburgh can spare you to America.

Imo   I don't belong to Aldeburgh. To anyone.

Ben   I played through everything I had of *Gloriana*. Up until act three scene one.

Imo   When was this, dear?

Ben   New Year's Eve. For George and Marion and Peter.

Imo   I'd wish I'd been there to hear it.

Ben   Peter's reconciled himself to playing Essex. Says will you coach him for the recorder part?

Imo   I'd be delighted. What did they all say when you played them *Gloriana*?

Ben   They all said it was marvellous.

Imo   As they should.

Ben   But I . . .

Imo   Yes?

Ben   I thought it was terribly monotonous.

Imo   It's not.

Ben   Where are the dynamics, the life?

Imo   There in abundance.

Ben   I'm the bloody composer, surely I know?

Imo   No you don't know. I know. I know that *Gloriana* is a terrific piece of work.

Ben   What if *Peter Grimes* was my great work and everything else is a dwindling?

Imo   Let's have more drink. One extraordinarily large rum and one elephantine Drambuie.

Ben   You'll send me to the Potters completely smashed.

Imo   Drive out the damp.

Ben   Here – guess what this is.

Ben *plays* Ride of the Valkyries *on the piano in a deliberately clumsy way.*

Ben   Have you guessed? It's Wagner after three rums.

Imo   Ha! Ha! Bravo.

Ben   Unt now – Wagner after six rums.

He plays even more clumsily.

Imo *claps.*

Ben   After twelve rums.

Ben *plays a crazy version of the Valkyries.* **Imo** *improvises a spear and a helmet and trots around the room.*

Ben   DEATH TO THE DEADLY DULL NINETEENTH CENTURY GERMANS!

Imo   BOO TO BEETHOVEN!

Ben   BUGGER OFF TO BRAHMS!

Imo   STUFF YOUR GESAMTKUNST WORK UP YOUR ARSEHOLE, WAGNER!

They both collapse into a fit of giggles.

Imo *pours them both another drink.*

Pause as they drink.

Ben   Imo –

Imo   Yes?

Ben   Peter's singing Bach cantatas. On the radio.

Imo   When?

Ben   Tonight.

Imo   Peter singing Bach. I wouldn't miss that for the world.

Ben   I don't want to sit with the Potters listening to Peter singing Bach. I want to listen with you.

Imo   I don't have a radio.

Ben   I could bring one to you. I don't mind sitting on the floor.

Imo   My room's terribly cold. It takes ages for the bar to heat up. I sleep under an old fur of mother's.

Ben   My astrakhan's very snug.

Imo   Do you miss Peter awfully when he's on tour?

Ben   He has to sing wherever he can. That's the most important thing.

Imo   I'd really like to get to know Peter better.

Ben   One can never really appreciate him enough, can one? How about I meet you here tonight? You wear your mother's fur, I'll wear the astrakhan. We'll light candles. You prepare something – coq au vin. Coq is in short supply but we'll make up for it with huge amounts of vin. Rum and Drambuie. And we'll listen to Peter sing Bach. What do you think?

Imo   I think, dear. I think. I won't come between you and Peter. You listen to the broadcast and I'll . . .

Ben   Sit in your garret and feel sorry for yourself?

Imo   Oh fuck off, dear, why don't you? I'll prepare for tomorrow. *Gloriana*.

Nine

Imo   Goodness. Twenty-eight pages. Twenty-eight pages. Twenty-eight –

Ben   Alright. Don't go on.

Imo   But Ben that is extraordinary! Twenty –

Ben   Eight pages, yes yes.

Imo   Of full orchestra score in one day. I don't think even Mozart –

Ben   Oh for God's sake, don't go comparing me with Mozart. I'm bound to be knocked out in the first round.

Imo   However did you do it?

Ben   I just – don't know – just wrote it.

Imo   Are you sure you haven't been hiding this away for weeks so that you could suddenly surprise me with your brilliance?

Ben   Wish I had. The truth is, Imo, I'm a very lazy sort of person.

Imo   Ttt!

Ben   I can sit around for weeks, months doing absolutely nothing.

Imo   I had noticed.

Ben   Walks, drives, films, gossip, Happy Families.

Imo   But maybe all the time your unconscious –

Ben   Well . . .

Imo   Your unconscious is sort of working away terribly hard, sorting everything out until finally –

Ben   Yes, I suppose that's it.

Imo   And then it all pops out when it's ready. When you played the piano and vocal to everyone at Covent Garden last week that was a sort of sign to your unconscious – here we go, let it all out. Full orchestral – here I come. I did think for a while: Why is he such a shirker and how the hell am I going to knock him into line? But now. Composers really are the most fascinating people that ever lived. I don't think I could ever tire of their minds.

Ben   Imo. Would you mind very much if we don't go on about my mind? Only I'd rather not look too deeply. I don't think I'd care too much for what I'd find there. Can we move on? Now I'm on a roll, I want to push through to the end.

Imo   Of course, yes. I shall have to race to keep up with you now, shan't I?

Ben   I suppose you rather will.

Imo   When one is assistant to a genius it's the genius who sets the pace. I hope I'm up to it, dear, a silly old woman.

Ben   Imo – can we cut out the prattling and get on with the work?

Imo   Yes, absolutely.

They sit either end of a table, **Imo** *copying from* **Ben***'s work. After a while:*

Ben   I've been thinking . . .

Imo   Yes?

Ben   The full orchestral will be done in a few weeks.

Imo   Sooner if you're working at this rate.

Ben   Your work on *Gloriana* will be finished.

Imo   I want to see her through to the opening. Maybe if I coached.

Ben   Coached?

Imo   If there were a small fee I could take some singers –

Ben   The musical assistant can't take the singers through their parts. That's an altogether different role.

Imo   Yes I suppose it is. What about the dance?

Ben   All sorted.

Imo   The little boy who dances the Morris. I could teach him. I'm very good with children.

Ben   I told you from the start: you mustn't claim on the boy. From the moment I conceived of the child –

Imo   You didn't – the child came about because I –

Ben   Imo! Don't! You're the musical assistant. You mustn't encroach. It always happens like this. It looks like I'll never write a thing and then suddenly it sort of pours and once it's all been poured then your job, Imo, is done. Just a couple more weeks and you'll be free.

Imo   Well, jolly good.

Ben   Let's make you a pot of money.

Imo   Money? How?

Ben   Send you off on that lecture tour of America. Big bucks. You can come back in time for the gala performance. Wearing jeans and chewing gum.

Imo   Ha!

They work for some time.

Ben   You alright, Imo?

Imo   What about my festival planning?

Ben   I've spoken to the committee. They'll push on without you.

Imo   I don't see how I –

Ben   I've drafted a letter of recommendation, scouted some introductions in the States. The path has been laid.

Imo   Oh.

Ben   Imo. Three months in America. Cash. Isn't that what you want?

Imo   It's what I said I wanted.

Ben   And now you've got what you said you wanted. I've arranged it. Aren't you going to thank me?

Imo   No, I'm not.

Ben   I see.

Imo   Well, you told me you'd do it. But I didn't listen. Not really.

Ben   What did I tell you?

Imo   That you'd pull me in, enchant me, love me then despise me, then push me away. And I suppose that's what's happened these six months, isn't it?

Ben   I have to work.

Imo   I thought there might be some drama about it. But in the end, all rather clinical. Job done old girl, well done, now off you piss.

Ten

Imo   I came to say goodbye.

Ben   I see, yes.

Imo   The boat for New York leaves at six this evening.

Ben   Goodbye.

Ben *keeps his head down in his work.*

Imo   The sea's much calmer now isn't it? I rather miss the storm. There was something beautiful about all that savagery.

Ben   Are you taking your three bags?

Imo   Yes, just the same three bags.

Ben   Very good.

Imo   Well, I mustn't interrupt you any longer.

Ben   I thought Pritchard might conduct *Gloriana*.

Imo   Pritchard?

Ben   I went to Covent Garden. Heard his *Norma*.

Imo   Bellini?

Ben   It was terrific.

Imo   But it's not Britten.

Ben   It's a grand opera. That's what *Gloriana* needs.

Imo   Well yes, I suppose Pritchard could conduct some of the performances. But you'll conduct the gala performance, won't you?

Ben   There are tunes in *Norma*. Real tunes.

Imo   I think we're all hoping that you'll conduct when the royals are in.

Ben   One day I'd like to write something with a really good tune.

Imo   Do you want to conduct the gala? You really must conduct it.

Ben   Pritchard's the man.

Imo   Oh no! Not Pritchard. Too romantic. No feel for Britten. You. The composer. You know your work far better than –

Ben   Imo! Go to America!

Imo   On my way. But before I leave I'm telling you what's best.

Ben   You're taking control. But I won't let you. You really can't be in charge of everything. You must allow me to decide some things for myself. And I've decided Pritchard.

Imo   Your mind's made up?

Ben   Completely made up.

Imo   I see. What a stupid, stubborn decision.

Ben   Piss off.

Imo   Well then. I best wend my merry, hadn't I?

Ben   Yes, you better. Imo . . .

Imo   Yes.

Ben   If I tell you a secret will you promise to keep it?

Imo   Of course.

Ben   Joan Cross came down yesterday.

Imo   I know. You were taking her through her part.

Ben   I've prepared Peter and Joan in some extracts. We're going to be singing a private preview for the Queen and Duke of Edinburgh. I wasn't supposed to tell anyone but –

Imo   When's the preview?

Ben   Tomorrow. The palace.

Imo   I see.

Ben   And I thought –

Imo   Don't.

Ben   If you were there turning the pages.

Imo   America.

Ben   I need you. Take the fear away.

Imo   It wouldn't be right. Old woman in a cardigan.

Ben   You'll scrub up. I know you will. One more day. I can call the agent, have you on to a ship as soon as we've played for the royals.

Imo   I have a speaking engagement in New York the day I land.

Ben   I'll have it moved.

Imo   No Ben, no. Stop it.

Ben   Imo – please!

Imo   No. I'm resolved. I'm leaving this morning.

Ben   Oh fuck.

Imo   I shall tell America all about you.

Ben   Now who's stubborn and stupid?

Imo   Goodbye dear. Break a leg at the palace.

Ben   You'll be back for June the eighth?

Imo   I don't think so.

Ben   The coronation gala. You must.

Imo   *Gloriana* will be your triumph, dear.

Ben   Our triumph.

Imo   No. Stop. Stop pretending. Let's both of us stop pretending. I won't be the phantom at the feast. I was outside the door yesterday.

Ben   Which door?

Imo   This door. I turned up and the door was closed. I was about to barge in then I heard. Ah! He's taking Joan Cross through her part. Elizabeth. Gloriana. And I said to myself: Listen. There. He had that passage when he first wrote it in altogether different key. And I said to him: That doesn't quite sit right. I mean it will 'do'. But it's not right. You seemed to ignore me. A few days later, you gave me the copy to work on – you didn't say anything – and – you'd changed it. New key. I stood yesterday in the corridor, wishing myself invisible, keeping my breath to almost nothing and just listened. And of course Joan was absolutely marvellous. You and Joan together were marvellous. Then I thought: Well – this it. This is the end for you, Imo old girl. Because did you really think that *Gloriana* was your own passion, yours and his? Imo and Ben. Because sometimes in this room. Working. It's felt like that hasn't it? But it's a grand opera. Benjamin Britten's coronation gala. Huge cast. There's Queen Elizabeth the Second, Harewood, Kenneth Clark, De Valois, Ashton. Plomer. Peter Pears – who you're in love with. I never wanted to be written into any of the big scenes. I'm a walk on. Lady in waiting. And my lines will get cut and cut. First the principals will gather. Then the chorus. Then the dancers. The orchestra. Then the audience. The royals and the great and the good. Until I'm a tiny little dot. Even if you want to talk to me – which I think you probably will – you shan't be able to because the noise will be too loud. I don't say this as a martyr dear. I say it because I have a clear eye. And on it will go. *Gloriana* will rush out in to the world. I read in the *Times* – you forgot to tell me, dear, too busy – that next season Maria Callas will sing *Gloriana* at La Scala. Time and again you've said – I know you have, dear, and I'm grateful – Imo, you're vital – I couldn't have done this without you. I heard the exact same tone in your voice yesterday. As you took Joan through her part. 'You're vital. I couldn't do this without you.' That's your cruelty. I see it now. You're very kind to whoever is most useful for your work. So now's the time for me to move on. Gypsy to America. I've done my work. I'm not a genius. There is genius. You have it. Being with you I've learnt: there's another quieter, duller, steadier personality without which genius is impossible. I am that other personality. I've made your genius possible and I'm proud to have played my part. Said my lines. You'll be remembered forever. I'll be forgot. As it should be. But *Gloriana* wouldn't have turned out the same if I wasn't here. I'll never tell anyone that. And I'd be grateful if you wouldn't blab about it either. Goodbye, dear Ben.

Ben   Oh Imo, not just yet. This whole coronation business has sent everyone mad. Booseys and Covent Garden have come up with an idea. They want the Queen to be presented with a specially bound edition of the vocal score. They want it to be presented to her at the gala performance. It's an awful problem. I don't want to settle on a final vocal score until I've heard a few performances. But it's my duty. Duty! It gets lodged forever. And then of course the Queen's vocal score shan't be right because I won't have heard the performances so then another, proper final vocal score will have to be written over the summer after the performances. I can't produce the vocal scores all by myself. I'll need someone.

Imo   Yes you will, dear. Only it won't be me.

Ben   Then who?

Imo   You'll find someone.

Imo   Who?

Imo   A musical assistant. Young and brilliant. I'll think about that on the train.

Ben   Alright.

Imo   I'll write you a list and post it when I get to the ship.

Ben   Thank you. Goodbye, dear.

Imo   Goodbye.

Ben *and* **Imo** *hug. A long time. Neither wants to let go.*

Imo   Goodbye.

Imo *exits.*

Ben *works on his orchestral score.*

Imo *returns.*

Imo   Damn you, Benjamin Britten. Damn your reedy voice, your piercing little eyes, and your clinging sticky arms.

Ben   Imo.

Imo   Damn your manipulations and games and cat and mouse.

Ben   What?

Imo   And damn me and my weakness. Because I understand exactly what's going on and yet.

Ben   You're staying?

Imo   Understand this: I'm a part of the making of *Gloriana* and I can't abandon her. I must see her through. I must copy every note and bar of every version of the score until she's fully done and out in to the world.

Imo *takes out her ticket.*

Ben   What's that?

Imo   My ticket to America.

Ben   I'll have it rearranged.

Imo   No. America is cancelled altogether.

Ben   But all I ask is that tomorrow –

Imo   And then another tomorrow. I'm not playing that game. I'm staying until the end.

Imo *begins to tear the ticket.*

Ben   Imo! You mustn't!

Imo   I won't be told what to do!

Imo *tears the ticket over and over until it's bits of confetti which she throws in the air.*

Imo   I'll start on the vocal score today.

Ben   It doesn't need to be so soon.

Imo   I'm staying to work.

Ben   You must come up to London with me today. I'm taking Peter and Joan through the whole opera. And then tomorrow the Queen.

Imo   I'm not interested in the Queen. I have to work on the vocal score.

Ben   I need you in London.

Imo   I can't be in two places at once. I'll stay in Aldeburgh. I'm the musical assistant.

Ben   But the Queen –

Imo   Stuff the Queen and fuck the Duke Edinburgh.

Ben   Imo!

Imo   Have you had your breakfast?

Ben   Mrs Hodson asked for the day off.

Imo   I'll need some fuel if I'm to start my work. My ring's playing up so I haven't had a thing.

Ben   I'm sure there's a bit of cheese and bread somewhere.

Imo   How about scrambled eggs?

Ben   If we have eggs.

Imo   Go and check, dear, and if there's eggs, give them a scramble while I start work. There's a dear.

Ben   If that's what you'd like.

Imo   It is.

Imo *crosses to the table and starts to study the* Gloriana *score.* **Ben** *watches her.*

Imo   Ben.

Ben   Yes?

Imo   Don't be disappointed.

Ben   Disappointed?

Imo   If tomorrow when you perform the extracts at the palace . . . don't be downhearted if the royals look a little – well – bored.

Ben   Bored? Do you think?

Imo   Bored or puzzled or perhaps even somewhat insulted.

Ben   Oh God.

Imo   Their emotions are stifled, their education limited. *Gloriana* is heart and brain while they . . .

Ben   Are you trying to frighten me?

Imo   Not frighten, no. Forewarn, forearm. Whatever happens – even if they – I don't know – nod off.

Ben   Stop!

Imo   Whatever the Queen and the Duke of Edinburgh do or say I want you to keep faith with your genius and with *Gloriana*. May I kiss you?

Ben   Why?

Imo   As a reminder tomorrow to believe in *Gloriana*.

Ben   Go on.

Ben *turns his cheek.* **Imo** *kisses it.*

Imo   How was that?

Ben   I won't scramble the eggs. If you want something, you must get it yourself.

Imo   Alright.

Ben   I only wanted you to stay for one more day.

Eleven

Imo   Sorry sorry sorry. Get my breath. Oh oh oh. Stich in my . . . Oh. My bike let me down. No repair kit for the puncture. So I – oh dear me. Not as fit as I. Could I – is there time? – sit for a moment? I know the driver's waiting outside but if I could just for a.

Ben *indicates to a chair.* **Imo** *sits.*

Imo   Any water? Doesn't matter. I barely slept. Did you sleep? The prospect of hearing *Gloriana* played by the orchestra of Covent Garden for the first time. It seemed almost criminal to sleep. I was awake until five. I was full of the most terrible imaginings. *Gloriana* in the hands of Pritchard. Said to myself: Face it, Imo – you won't sleep, get out of bed right now. The next thing I knew it was seven-forty. I ran through the town. Do I look ridiculous? No time to brush my hair. Do I look like a madwoman? They should be used to madwomen in opera houses shouldn't they? Should I brush my hair? I think it's best if I brush my hair. I don't want the driver to see. I'm not sure I've got – it might be . . .

Imo *searches in her bag.*

How do you think Pritchard will do? I worry that he hasn't prepared enough. Aha! Hairbrush. You're so terribly brave. Just handing the orchestral over to a conductor like that. When every bar is infused with your being and you could communicate that so wonderfully to the orchestra yourself. I know not the performance itself but I thought for the orchestral you might . . . One doesn't like to step on Pritchard's toes but I thought you might. Ben? Ben! Say something. I know you're angry, dear and I don't expect you to forgive me for being so horribly late. But if you could just look at me. Look at me, Ben. I've never been late any other day. Although I know that this day is more important than any other day.

Ben The piss pot's gone.

Imo What?

Ben The Lord Chamberlain's banned the piss pot from *Gloriana*.

Imo I see.

Ben He's allowed everything else. But he's put a firm pencil through the piss pot.

Imo Oh dear.

Ben Harewood made enquiries. Quiet word. Was it this particular piss pot? Was it having a piss pot in a scene in an opera about a Queen? Or was it that our young Elizabeth will be watching *Gloriana* and she might be offended by the sight of a piss pot? I suppose, don't you, that the Queen must take a piss from time to time?

Imo I'm sure she must.

Ben And I imagine – all those long corridors, middle of the night – she must keep under her bed – perhaps a very old, perhaps made for Queen Anne – piss pot.

Imo Almost certainly.

Ben   But the Lord Chamberlain said no. It wasn't the *Gloriana* piss pot that he objects to. It's piss pots in general. No piss pot is ever to be allowed on a British stage. The piss pot must remain forever in the wings. What do you think of that?

Imo   I suppose –

Ben   I think it's funny.

Imo   Do you?

Ben   Terribly funny.

Imo   Then so do I.

Ben   Shall we get in the car?

Imo   The rain's cleared. We'll make it to Covent Garden just in time. And I really am sorry about . . .

Ben   As a matter of fact.

Imo   Yes?

Ben   I've decided to conduct the first half hour of the orchestral myself.

Imo   Really?

Ben   Really.

Imo   Oh Ben! That's wonderful. Now everything's going to be alright. I know it is. I should have slept like a babe and been as punctual as a pea if I'd known. That will give the orchestra the lead / however much Pritchard mangles.

Ben   FOR FUCK'S SAKE, SHUT UP, WOMAN! SHUT UP TELLING ME WHAT TO DO!

Pause.

Imo   I'm sorry. I'm sorry that I've made you so angry on this important day.

Ben   You think I want to hear what you have to say. I don't.
You don't control anything. It's an opera. Composer.
Conductor. Orchestra. We each have our jobs to do. We must
each keep in our place. Your place is to look after the score,
take your notes, do your job and until you're asked to speak,
keep your fucking mouth shut.

Imo   I've failed you.

Ben   Are you grizzling yet? Like a school girl? No? Oh your
eyes are still dry. Well, I shall have to do something about
that, shan't I? I simply want you to do your job. And all you
had to do today was to turn up with your notebook. On
time. And you couldn't even do that. Today an opera is being
born and you're not its father or its mother, nor its aunt or
its grandmother. You're not even the midwife. And you're
certainly not a lady in waiting. So what are you? I'll tell you
what you are. You're the dim-witted servant girl. The girl
who – when the time's due – has a simple job: to run to the
midwife. And now what do I discover? You can't even
fucking well do that. 'Oh sorry sir I forgot to run for the
midwife. Why sir? Well, because, sir, I'm just too bloody
stupid, sir.' And if today my little opera dies before it
properly leaves the womb, who'll be to blame? The dim-
witted servant girl. And if that happens, I shall have you
pulled out in front of all the others and I shall thrash you
until your skin breaks and bleeds.

Imo *lets out a sob.*

Ben   You're breaking. Breaking. Tears on the way. I knew I
could do it. I'll make you weep. You'll howl. I won't be like
your father. I won't be Gustav Holst. One piece, one! Only
one piece of Holst's will be remembered. One piece played
all over the world. And everything else – however much it
was fussed over and petted and promoted by his beloved
daughter – every other piece – slung in the rubble with the
rest of all the not good enough art. Forgotten. Who knows?
Without you as his gaoler Holst might have written better
and better –

Imo   SHUT UP! SHUT UP!

Ben   You won't hold me back, Imogen Holst. I won't
dwindle. You won't pull me down in to your inheritance of
the second rate!

Imo   PLEASE!

Ben   Not such a coper as you think are, eh? Weak. Broken.

Pause.

Ben   Oh, Imo, why am I so cruel?

Imo   I suppose because it's your time to push me away.

Ben   At the palace, Joan and Peter sang beautifully. And the
royals – you were right – thoroughly bored. They could
hardly wait for it to be over. They're not bred for emotion.
They wear a mask. War or peace, abdication or coronation,
Churchill or Attlee – they have to make sure that the voice
and the face remain exactly the same. The gloved hand
might applaud but it will never make a sound. Nine months
of wasted work. *Gloriana* is going to be a huge disaster. We
fought a war for civilisation and out of that there's a new
hunger for music in this country, we're actually getting the
government to spend proper money on the arts, for the first
time we have a national opera. I can see our future: great big
national buildings, great big national companies, huge
enormous sensational international stars and huge great big
international works of art. And I don't want any of it. So . . .
what? Back to Aldeburgh. Back to writing for my friends.
With our little opera group every year looking glumly at its
pocket book with figures written in red ink. All the time
trying to scrape together enough money to put on the next
little piece. Hand to mouth. I'm not a national person. I'm a
local person. I'm small halls and small works with people
who I know and who love the work. That's what feels safest.
Is safety the mother of art? Am I scared of working with the
very best? When I'd finished playing *Gloriana* – that room in
the palace – I looked at Elizabeth and Phillip. The Queen.

The Duke of Edinburgh. The new Elizabethan age. I saw dull eyes and dull minds and dull hearts. And that's what there'll be in their opera houses of the future: huge great audiences of thousands upon thousands brought together by their dullness.

Imo   What's next?

Ben   Next?

Imo   What opera will you write next for Peter and Joan?

Ben   I don't know.

Imo   Yes you do.

Ben   I know I shan't ever write a grand opera again. Imo, I'm sorry I – if you want to – go.

Imo   Where would I go?

Ben   Back to bed, go to your mother. America.

Imo   *Turn of the Screw*'s the next opera to be written. The Venice festival want it for next year. Peter told me.

Ben   I should be in the car.

Imo   *Turn of the Screw*'s what you really wanted to write all along, isn't it?

Ben   If I'm to make it to the orchestral rehearsal.

Imo   Covent Garden can wait until the composer is ready. It'll give Pritchard a bit of time to study his score. You'd have written *Turn of the Screw* by now if Harewood and Kenneth Clark hadn't got at you. Pushed you in to their pompous notion of a coronation opera.

Ben   It was my choice.

Imo   No. Not your choice. You were weak. Betrayed your instinct. That was a very silly thing to do. I agree. *Gloriana* will be a huge disaster. June the eighth. All those lords and ladies will turn their noses in disgust at the bald, arrogant

old Queen up there on the stage. The coronation gala
performance will be the punishment for all your cruelty. You
shouldn't be writing grand opera. La Scala. Callas. It's not
for you. The smaller forces of the *Turn of the Screw* will be
much better suited to Benjamin Britten. Where's your copy
of the novella, dear? I'm sure I saw it somewhere here
amongst the terrible mess of your desk. Aha!

Imo *locates* The Turn of the Screw.

Imo (*reading from the book*)   'I remember the whole
beginning as a succession of flights and drops, a little seesaw
of the right throbs and the wrong.'

Ben   What are you doing?

Imo   I'm reading you *Turn of the Screw*. It's not very long.
I'll read it all the way through out loud in the car up to
London.

Ben   I'll want to study my *Gloriana* score in the car up to
London.

Imo   Study *Gloriana*? You know *Gloriana* inside out. No
need to study *Gloriana*. On to the next opera. On to *Turn of
the Screw*. I'm ready to go now. Where have you left your
coat?

Ben   I shouldn't have said . . . all those horrible.

Imo   No. You shouldn't. But it's said now. Come on. Peter
will fret if he doesn't see your face.

Ben   So what do we . . .? Is everything forgotten? My
cruelty. And forgiven.

Imo   No. Not forgotten. Not forgiven.

Ben   I promise I'll never speak to you like that ever again.

Imo   I'll make sure you shan't. Working on *Gloriana* I
allowed myself to become . . . I showed too much of myself.
My heart. When we work on *Turn of the Screw* I'll make sure I
keep my distance.

Ben   You're staying to work on *Turn of the Screw*?

Imo   Of course I'm staying to work on *Turn of the Screw*.

Ben   Why?

Imo   Because you'll need a musical assistant. And there's no one better than me.

Ben   You don't have to, Imo.

Imo   I want to.

Ben   Now's your chance to escape.

Imo   Because you've decided that it's time to push me away? No. I won't be pushed away. I shall stay in Aldeburgh. 1954. Fifty-five. Fifty-six. Forever. And a day. I shall always remember your cruelty. I shall always remember that today I've seen you as you truly are. And you won't forget either. You'll always know that I've seen your true self. Which gives me a sort of power doesn't it? I've been working through *Gloriana*.

Ben   Whatever for?

Imo   I've made an arrangement of music from the Masque.

Ben   No no.

Imo   For voice. The concert platform. I thought I'd call it *Choral Dances*. I've brought you the arrangement. Would you take a look at it? Not now. Once we've got through June the eighth.

Imo *takes the* Choral Dances *manuscript from her bag, puts it on* **Ben**'s *desk.*

Ben   Once we're through June the eighth, I intend to forget all about *Gloriana*.

Imo   Ben, *Gloriana* is a very fine opera. Only this isn't its time. You won't get a proper revival for God knows how long. But you will eventually and then everyone will see that *Gloriana* is a wonderful piece. But until then I shall arrange selections from *Gloriana*, conduct selections from *Gloriana*. I shall slip *Gloriana*, bit by bit, into whatever programme I can. Until she springs back again in to glorious life. Now put your coat on, dear, and let's motor up to Covent Garden and hold dear old *Gloriana*'s hand as she mounts the scaffold, puts her head on the block, and feels the axe fall.

Ben   I'm frightened.

Imo   I know.

Ben   Hold me.

Imo   No.

End.

For a complete listing of
Methuen Drama titles, visit:
www.bloomsbury.com/drama

Follow us on Twitter and keep up to date
with our news and publications
@MethuenDrama